United States Government Accountability Office

Report to Congressional Requesters

November 2013

DEFENSE LOGISTICS

Army Should Track Financial Benefits Realized from its Logistics Modernization Program

GAO-14-51

November 2013

DEFENSE LOGISTICS

Army Should Track Financial Benefits Realized from its Logistics Modernization Program

GAO Highlights

Highlights of GAO-14-51, a report to congressional requesters

Why GAO Did This Study

LMP is an Army enterprise resource planning system that supports industrial operations conducted by AMC at its life cycle management commands and its maintenance, manufacturing, and storage sites. Increment 1 of LMP was fully deployed in October 2010, and the Army has spent approximately $1.4 billion on LMP through fiscal year 2012. In order to expand the system's capabilities, the Army plans to deploy a second increment of LMP. The life cycle cost for LMP Increment 1 and Increment 2, from fiscal year 2000 through 2026, is estimated to be over $4 billion. GAO was asked to evaluate AMC's use of LMP. This report assesses the extent to which (1) LMP supports AMC's industrial operations and (2) the Army has realized the expected benefits from deploying LMP. GAO reviewed Army documents regarding LMP usage and interviewed officials from AMC headquarters, the LMP product office, and 14 AMC sites that use LMP to conduct their operations.

What GAO Recommends

To enable the Army to determine whether the expected financial benefits of LMP are being achieved, GAO recommends that the Army develop and implement a process to track the extent of financial benefits realized from the use of LMP during the remaining course of its life cycle. This process should be linked with the LMP performance baseline now being developed by the Army for use at AMC industrial sites. The Army concurred with GAO's recommendation.

View GAO-14-51. For more information, contact Zina Merritt at (202) 512-5257 or merrittz@gao.gov.

What GAO Found

The Army Materiel Command (AMC) is using the Logistics Modernization Program (LMP) Increment 1 to support its industrial operations, but additional development is necessary, according to the Army, because the current system does not support certain critical requirements, including enabling the Army to generate auditable financial statements by fiscal year 2017. Officials at the 14 AMC sites GAO visited stated that LMP provided the core functionality they needed to support their operations and that they are improving in their ability to use the system. Additionally, some sites have locally developed tools to augment LMP capabilities. Army officials stated that although LMP is functional, it currently does not support certain critical requirements that have emerged since its initial development, such as automatically tracking repair and manufacturing operations on the shop floor of depots and arsenals. In addition, according to Army officials, the current system will not enable the Army to generate auditable financial statements by 2017, the statutory deadline for this goal. Increment 2, which is estimated to cost $730 million through fiscal year 2026, is expected to address these shortcomings. The Army is in the process of developing Increment 2 and expects to complete fielding by September 2016.

The use of LMP Increment 1 has provided the Army some benefits, but whether the system has delivered the expected financial benefits to date is unknown because AMC does not have a process for tracking financial benefits realized. Since its deployment, LMP has provided some benefits to the Army. For example, because LMP relies on accurate data to perform effectively and efficiently, the Army has made data accuracy a priority and improved the accuracy of its data by conducting data assessments, correcting data problems, and placing management emphasis on data accuracy. Additionally, the use of LMP has improved accountability for inventory stored at AMC depots, increased visibility over Army assets, and resulted in other efficiencies—such as providing faster access to information. AMC officials also stated that LMP has enabled them to develop and begin to implement a set of standardized, enterprise-wide performance measures to better assess the business operations of AMC sites. The officials stated that these performance measures, which were being used during AMC leadership reviews in June 2013, were necessary because the measures previously used to assess AMC performance were inadequate. However, the extent to which financial benefits have been realized from deploying LMP is unknown. The Army expected LMP to lead to over $750 million in financial benefits by fiscal year 2012 and eventually achieve more than two dollars in benefits for every dollar spent. Army officials told us that there currently is no accurate process in place to track financial benefits associated with LMP. Officials stated that the inability to quantify benefits from LMP-driven performance improvements was due in part to the fluctuations in AMC workload resulting from operations in Iraq and Afghanistan. The Army is in the process of developing a performance baseline for sites that will pilot Increment 2, and it intends to apply these metrics to other AMC sites before May 2015. Federal guidelines and standards outline the need for assessing whether the benefits expected from an investment are achieved. Without a process in place to track the financial benefits associated with LMP, the Army does not have a way to determine whether LMP's projected financial benefits are materializing.

United States Government Accountability Office

Contents

Letter		1
	Background	3
	LMP Supports AMC's Industrial Operations, but Additional Development Is Needed to Meet Certain Critical Requirements	6
	LMP Has Provided Some Benefits to the Army, but the Extent of Financial Benefits to Date Is Unknown	15
	Conclusions	22
	Recommendation for Executive Action	22
	Agency Comments and Our Evaluation	23

Appendix I	Scope and Methodology	24

Appendix II	Comments from the Department of the Army	26

Appendix III	GAO Contact and Staff Acknowledgments	28

Related GAO Products		29

Tables

	Table 1: Estimated Total Life Cycle Costs of LMP Increments 1 and 2, Fiscal Year 2000–2026	6
	Table 2: LMP Increment 2 Components and Deployment Timeline	11
	Table 3: Projected Financial Benefits from LMP Increment 2	14

Figure

	Figure 1: LMP Development and Deployment Timeline	5

Abbreviations

AMC	Army Materiel Command
LMP	Logistics Modernization Program

November 13, 2013

The Honorable Robert Wittman
Chairman
The Honorable Madeleine Z. Bordallo
Ranking Member
Subcommittee on Readiness
Committee on Armed Services
House of Representatives

The Honorable J. Randy Forbes
House of Representatives

The Army's Logistics Modernization Program (LMP) is among a new
generation of enterprise resource planning systems[1] that are replacing
older legacy systems in the Department of Defense (DOD). The Army
initiated LMP in 1999 and completed final deployment of Increment 1 of
the system in 2010. LMP is deployed at about 50 industrial operations
sites within Army Materiel Command (AMC), including its life cycle
management commands, maintenance depots, arsenals, and ammunition
manufacturing and storage sites and has over 20,000 users. As of fiscal
year 2012, the Army had spent $1.4 billion on LMP. The Army projected
that LMP would provide over $750 million in financial benefits by fiscal
year 2012 through, for example, reducing inventory and legacy system
costs.[2]

---

[1] An enterprise resource planning system is an automated information system using
commercial off-the-shelf software and consisting of multiple, integrated functional modules
that perform a variety of business-related tasks such as accounting; inventory forecasting,
purchasing, management, and distribution; and scheduling work.

[2] This projection is from an Army study prepared by the LMP program office and reviewed
by the Deputy Assistant Secretary of the Army for Cost and Economics to support the
fiscal year 2010 Investment Review Board certification of LMP. Investment Review Board
Certification is required for certain information technology programs with investment costs
of $1 million or more. The certification package includes a section on the economic
viability of the investment, to include the benefit-to-cost ratio and the return on investment.

We have conducted several prior reviews that identified weaknesses in the Army's planning and deployment of LMP.[3] In our most recent review, in November 2010, we reported that it was unclear whether the system would provide sites with all the software functionality they needed to conduct their operations, whether data maintained in the system were sufficiently accurate, and whether the Army would achieve all the expected benefits from its investment in the system.[4] Given the long-standing challenges associated with the Army's deployment of LMP, we recommended that the Army provide periodic reports to Congress on the progress of LMP deployment, the costs of addressing missing LMP functionality, and the benefits gained from using LMP. Although DOD concurred with our recommendation, it has not yet provided any such reports to Congress.

In response to your request that we evaluate AMC's use of LMP, this report assesses the extent to which (1) LMP supports AMC's industrial operations and (2) the Army has realized the expected benefits from deploying LMP.

To assess the extent to which LMP supports AMC's industrial operations, we met with and obtained information from Army officials who are responsible for implementing and overseeing LMP. We reviewed status reports that had been submitted to AMC headquarters by subordinate commands and individual sites. We visited 14 AMC sites where the system is deployed, including all five Army life cycle management commands, all five Army depots, one Army arsenal, and three ammunition sites. We also reviewed our prior work related to the deployment of LMP and followed up on issues that we had previously identified. We obtained information from AMC and the LMP product office on the Army's future plans for LMP and reviewed key documents, such as the business case and an accompanying economic analysis, that were

---

[3]See Related GAO Products at the end of this report. The Department of Defense Inspector General (DODIG) has also performed reviews of LMP to assess whether the system properly supports DOD business processes (see DODIG, *Logistics Modernization Program System Procure-to-Pay Process Did Not Correct Material Weaknesses*, DODIG-2012-087, May 29, 2012), as well as reviews of the Army's ability to meet financial improvement and audit readiness goals (see DODIG, *Enterprise Resource Planning Systems Schedule Delays and Weaknesses Increase Risks to DOD's Auditability Goals*, DODIG-2012-111, Jul. 13, 2012).

[4]GAO, *Defense Logistics: Additional Oversight and Reporting for the Army Logistics Modernization Program Are Needed*, GAO-11-139 (Washington, D.C.: Nov. 18, 2010).

developed to support expanded capabilities to the system. To determine the extent to which the Army has realized expected benefits from deploying LMP, we reviewed pertinent Army documents that outlined the expected financial benefits from deploying LMP. We requested information from AMC, the LMP product office, and individual AMC sites that we visited regarding actual benefits, if any, achieved to date. Appendix I provides further information on our scope and methodology.

We conducted this performance audit from August 2012 to November 2013 in accordance with generally accepted government auditing standards. Those standards require that we plan and perform the audit to obtain sufficient, appropriate evidence to provide a reasonable basis for our findings and conclusions based on our audit objectives. We believe that the evidence obtained provides a reasonable basis for our findings and conclusions based on our audit objectives.

Background

The Army initiated LMP in 1999 to replace two aging materiel management systems—the Commodity Command Standard System and the Standard Depot System. In replacing these systems, which had been used for more than 30 years to manage inventory, depot maintenance, and arsenal manufacturing operations, the Army expected LMP to help transform its logistics operations. A modified commercial off-the-shelf system, LMP was intended to support AMC industrial operations and improve business processes and practices in areas such as operations at depots and arsenals and inventory management. By providing a single source of data and integrated decision-making tools, LMP was expected to increase efficiencies in AMC operations—such as buying and managing spare and repair parts and conducting depot level maintenance. For example, in the area of planning future maintenance capacity, the Army expected improvements to AMC budget forecasts and adjustments through reduced repair cycle time, better resource allocation, increased production throughput, reduced production cost, and more accurate production schedules. With LMP's deployment, the Army expected to achieve benefits that included reduced equipment repair times, improved inventory forecasting, and cost savings. Additionally, LMP is part of the Army's broader strategy to implement enterprise resource planning systems in other areas and, as such, is expected to integrate with other Army systems, to include the General Fund

Enterprise Business System and the Global Combat Support System-Army.[5]

The deployment of LMP Increment 1 across AMC occurred in three phases between 2003 and 2010. The first phase of LMP deployment occurred at the Communications-Electronics Command and Tobyhanna Army Depot in July 2003. LMP was originally expected to be fully deployed across AMC by June 2004, but problems experienced during the first phase of deployment caused the Army to delay further deployment until these problems were resolved. The second phase of LMP deployment occurred at the Aviation and Missile Command and Corpus Christi and Letterkenny Army Depots in May 2009. The third and final deployment phase occurred in October 2010 at depots, arsenals, and other sites within the Army Sustainment Command, the Joint Munitions and Lethality Command, and the Tank-automotive and Armaments Command.

The Army has plans to expand the capabilities of LMP. On December 27, 2011, the Under Secretary of Defense for Acquisition, Technology and Logistics signed an Acquisition Decision Memorandum that categorized the deployed components of LMP as Increment 1 and considered all new LMP acquisition activities after December 28, 2011, to be Increment 2. The memorandum directed the Army, in preparing for the next acquisition milestone review of Increment 2, to submit an updated business case along with other specified documents. The Army prepared and submitted documents in response to the memorandum, including an updated business case[6] and an accompanying economic analysis,[7] for an

---

[5]By the fourth quarter of fiscal year 2017, all three of these enterprise resource planning systems are expected to be fully deployed, to share a common set of data, and to be able to provide the Army complete visibility over the wholesale and retail levels of supply.

[6]U.S. Army Program Executive Officer for Enterprise Information Systems, *Army Logistics Modernization Program (LMP) Increment 2 Business Case for Milestone B*, Aug. 2013. The business case was approved by the LMP Product Director and other Army offices, including AMC, the Program Executive Officer for Enterprise Information Systems, and the Assistant Deputy Chief of Staff, G-4.

[7]U.S. Army Program Executive Officer for Enterprise Information Systems, *Army Logistics Modernization Program (LMP) Increment 2 Economic Analysis (EA)* Aug. 2013. The purpose of the economic analysis was to discuss and compare the costs and benefits of maintaining the status quo and implementing LMP Increment 2. Similar to the business case, the economic analysis was approved by Army offices, including the LMP Product Director.

acquisition milestone review that was held on June 25, 2013. As a result of this review, the Army received approval for Increment 2 to move into the engineering development phase of its acquisition.[8] The Army intends to deploy Increment 2 in three waves, beginning in December 2013, and is planning for the deployment to be completed by September 30, 2016. Figure 1 shows a timeline for LMP development and deployment, including both Increment 1 and Increment 2.

Figure 1: LMP Development and Deployment Timeline

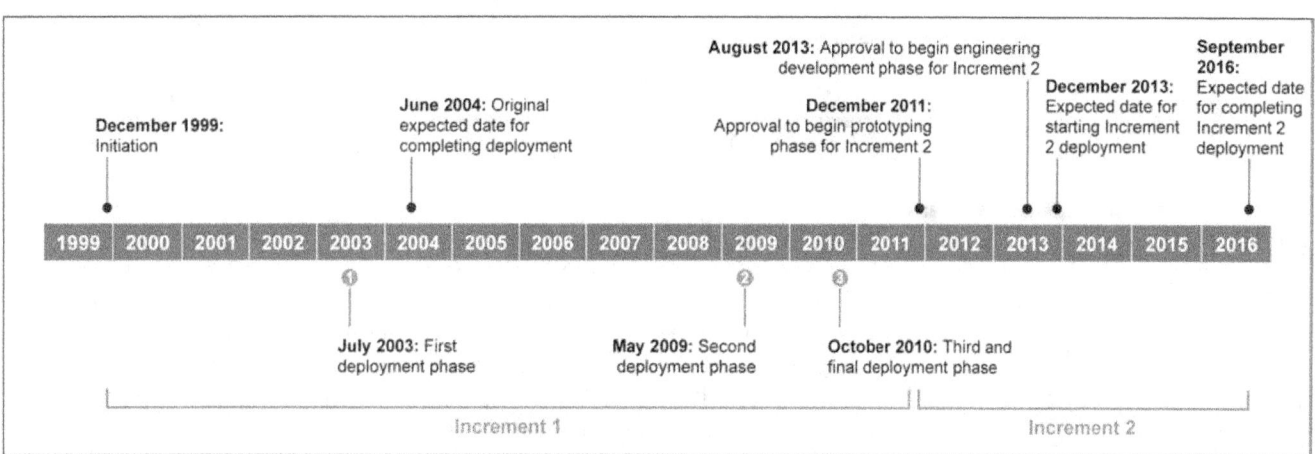

Source: GAO analysis of Army data.

As of May 2013, the Army had increased its projections for the system's total life cycle costs from $2.6 billion (fiscal years 2000 through 2021) to more than $4 billion (fiscal years 2000 through 2026). This estimate includes the fielded components of LMP—Increment 1—as well as the expansion of LMP capabilities under Increment 2 (see table 1).

---

[8]The purpose of engineering development is to demonstrate that the solution is ready for limited fielding and testing in an operational environment. See DOD Directive-Type Memorandum (DTM) 11-009, *Acquisition Policy for Defense Business Systems (DBS)*.

Table 1: Estimated Total Life Cycle Costs of LMP Increments 1 and 2, Fiscal Year 2000–2026

Dollars in millions

Fiscal year	Increment 1	Increment 2	Total
2000-2012	1,388.2	17.3	1,405.5
2013	236.6	109.0	345.6
2014	226.8	125.2	352.0
2015	162.0	125.2	287.2
2016	159.6	83.3	242.9
2017-2026	1,155.0	269.7	1,424.7
Total	**3,328.2**	**729.7**	**4,057.9**

Source: GAO summary of Army data.

LMP Supports AMC's Industrial Operations, but Additional Development Is Needed to Meet Certain Critical Requirements

AMC is using LMP to support its industrial operations, but additional development of LMP is necessary, according to the Army, because the current system does not support certain critical requirements that have emerged since the initial development of LMP and because the current system will not enable the Army to generate auditable financial statements. Officials at the 14 AMC sites we visited stated that LMP provided the core functionality they needed to support their operations. They stated that over time they are improving in their ability to use LMP, and some sites have locally developed tools to augment its capabilities. Army officials stated that although LMP is functional, the current system does not support certain critical requirements, such as requirements related to automatically tracking repair and manufacturing operations on the shop floor of depots and arsenals. In addition, according to Army officials, the current system will not enable the Army to generate financial statements validated as ready for audit by 2017, the statutory deadline for this goal. Increment 2 is intended to address these shortcomings.

AMC Is Using LMP to Support Its Industrial Operations

AMC is using LMP to support operations at its industrial sites. Officials at all 14 of the sites we visited between October 2012 and March 2013 told us that LMP provided the core functionality they needed to conduct their operations. Specifically, officials from each of the five Army depots stated that they were able to perform their maintenance, repair, and overhaul responsibilities using LMP; Rock Island Arsenal officials stated that they could perform their manufacturing operations using LMP; and officials at the Army ammunition sites we visited told us they used LMP to manage their inventory. Similarly, officials at the life cycle management commands stated that they were able to carry out their operations, which include the management of spare parts inventory. Additionally, periodic status reports submitted to AMC headquarters show that industrial sites where LMP has been deployed have been able to conduct their repair and manufacturing operations. These reports—which include data on the workload planned and completed for the current fiscal year—are submitted and discussed during regularly-held meetings to provide AMC headquarters with an update on the status of operations. Furthermore, the Army's fiscal year 2013 and 2014 working capital fund budget documents state that LMP is functional at each of AMC's life cycle management commands.

We reported in November 2010 that the Army Sustainment Command, the Joint Munitions and Lethality Command, and arsenals under the Tank-automotive and Armaments Command—all of which had been in the final deployment phase of LMP in October 2010—required additional system functionality to perform their unique operations and that this functionality had not yet been delivered.[9] We followed up on each of these previously reported issues for our current review.

- The Army Sustainment Command needed (1) an interface between LMP and the Army War Reserve Deployment System, a separate system used to track inventory and transfer accountability of pre-positioned stocks to units and (2) software functionality to conduct mass uploads—the automated movement of thousands of items of inventory between the Army Sustainment Command and the warfighter. During our current review, we found that the Army Sustainment Command had established an interface between LMP and the Army War Reserve Deployment System, and officials stated that LMP now has the capability to perform a mass upload.

- The Joint Munitions and Lethality Command required specific functionality to ship, receive, inventory, and perform stock movements for ammunition. To accomplish these tasks, the Joint Munitions and Lethality Command required the development of an interface between LMP and a system commonly referred to as SmartChain.[10] We found

---

[9]GAO-11-139.

[10]SmartChain is a software application that interfaces with LMP to provide an electronic method for performing standard depot operations such as receiving, moving, inventorying, and shipping ammunition. It tracks, automates, and integrates depot operations to manage and update inventory records.

during our current review that the interface between LMP and SmartChain has been established, and officials stated that LMP and SmartChain provide the capability needed to perform these tasks.[11]

- The Tank-automotive and Armaments Command required specific functionality at its arsenals to automatically report data for items it manufactures. When Rock Island Arsenal and Watervliet Arsenal switched from their legacy system to LMP, they lost this capability because LMP does not include a manufacturing and execution system that provides this capability. We found during our current review that Rock Island Arsenal has since developed its own software tools and manual processes to provide similar functionality. Specifically, Rock Island Arsenal uses three legacy systems, which together cost approximately $300,000 per year to operate. Arsenal officials told us that they developed an additional system to report manufacturing data and track the status of items being manufactured—at a cost of about $400,000. They hired additional personnel to manage these systems, which includes manually entering data into LMP. According to documents provided by Rock Island officials, annual costs for these systems and personnel will average $3.6 million from fiscal years 2013 through 2016. Arsenal and AMC officials stated that they expect Increment 2 to replace systems they are currently using to manage their shop floor operations. (We did not visit Watervliet Arsenal for this review).

Officials at AMC sites we visited stated that over time they are improving in their ability to use LMP, and some locations have developed tools and processes to better extract and analyze LMP data, or to fill in gaps in existing LMP functionality. In addition to the manufacturing tracking tools and processes developed at Rock Island Arsenal, as discussed above, we found the following examples:

- Red River Army Depot officials created a tool that enables users to generate customizable reports based on data extracted from LMP. Officials said they use these reports to brief depot leadership on areas such as schedule performance and inventory. Tobyhanna Army Depot created a tool using Microsoft Excel that extracts data from LMP and develops visual reports—in graphs and charts—to analyze depot

---

[11]We have ongoing work looking at visibility that LMP and other information systems provide over the conventional ammunition inventory.

workload and perform capacity planning. According to Tobyhanna officials, these reports allow them to manage depot operations by, for example, determining whether workload schedules need to be adjusted or personnel reassigned to higher priority tasks.[12]

- Corpus Christi Army Depot, using a combination of legacy systems, manual processes, and a locally-developed software tool, gained, among other things, the ability to automatically track the progress of work on the shop floor and record employee's labor charges. Depot officials stated that the use of this tool, in conjunction with LMP, has provided them with detailed data that helps them to better manage their operations and achieve efficiencies by improving depot processes, such as decreasing the cost to repair UH-60 helicopters (from $7.58 million per helicopter in fiscal year 2011 to $6.82 million per helicopter in fiscal year 2012) while increasing the quantity of UH-60 helicopters they can repair (from 48 in fiscal year 2011 to 51 in fiscal year 2012).

Additional LMP Development Needed to Meet Certain Critical Army Requirements

The Army is continuing development of LMP because, as currently deployed, it does not provide all of the functionality the Army needs to meet certain critical requirements, according to Army officials. According to the Army's business case for Increment 2, the new functionality the Army is developing as part of Increment 2 is intended to address critical requirements that have emerged since the initial development of LMP and that are not addressed by Increment 1. The business case stated that the current system does not support certain critical AMC requirements pertaining to shop floor automation, Army business transformation goals (for example, maintaining data on the maintenance status of equipment), and requirements outlined in DOD guidance (for example, requirements

---

[12]The reports produced by Tobyhanna depict workforce and workload data in graphs similar to those created by the Army Workload and Performance System, which is a separate information system that receives data from other systems—primarily LMP—to produce management reports and decision support tools intended to assist AMC sites in linking their workload demands to their workforce requirements. For more information on this system, see GAO, *Defense Logistics: Oversight and a Coordinated Strategy Needed to Implement the Army Workload and Performance System*, GAO-11-566R (Washington, D.C.: Jul. 14, 2011). In addition, we have begun a new engagement that will compare the management support and reporting capabilities of the Army Workload and Performance System with those available through LMP.

related to item unique identification[13]). Requirements for Increment 2 can be categorized into six components: (1) further integration with other Army and Defense Logistics Agency enterprise resource planning systems, (2) controlling and maintaining visibility over material managed by non-Army sources of supply, (3) additional capability to manage Army prepositioned stocks, (4) managing repair operations at Army installations, (5) expanded ammunition management capability, and (6) tracking repair and manufacturing operations on the shop floor. Table 2 summarizes the six components and the time line for their deployment.

---

[13]Item unique identification refers to technology that allows DOD to assign a unique number to an individual item and then use that unique number to manage the item in a variety of logistics processes. For further information on the status of this technology in DOD, see GAO, *Defense Logistics: Improvements Needed to Enhance DOD's Management Approach and Implementation of Item Unique Identification Technology*, GAO-12-482 (Washington, D.C.: May 3, 2012).

Table 2: LMP Increment 2 Components and Deployment Timeline

Component	Business need to be addressed	Expected Users	Timeline
Enterprise Resource Planning System Integration	Enhancing the interchange of data with other Army and Defense Logistics Agency enterprise resource planning systems.	Primarily a technical release; not deployed to specific sites; no new users.	December 2013 through July 2014
Non-Army Managed Items	Replacing the last instance of the legacy Commodity Command Standard System that supports Army-owned Non-Army Managed Items and improving overall inventory management.	Approximately 36 item managers at the Tank-automotive and Armaments Command.	August 2014 through September 2015
Army Prepositioned Stock	Modernizing the manually intensive war reserves planning process, which is currently performed outside of LMP.	Approximately 100 users that manage Army Prepositioned Stock.	August 2014 through September 2015
National Maintenance Program	Integrating the work loading and management processes of LMP Increment 1 with the system that will be used to execute below-depot maintenance at Army installations.	Approximately 200 users at the AMC life cycle management commands who manage the national maintenance program.	May 2015 through September 2016
Extended Ammunition	Improving AMC national-level ammunition management processes that currently require multiple systems, including LMP Increment 1, to receive, store, survey, and issue ammunition. The use of multiple systems causes timing issues, impacting real-time visibility and accountability of ammunition assets.	Approximately 1,500 users in the Joint Munitions and Lethality Command.	May 2015 through September 2016
Expanded Industrial Base	Automating shop floor operations that currently may rely on paper, manual data collection, and complicated processes. Also fulfills a need to improve management of Army military equipment and a DOD requirement to implement item unique identification capability.	Approximately 12,200 users (8,700 new users) at the 17 industrial base sites.	May 2015 through September 2016

Source: GAO summary of Army business case.

In addition to the critical requirements identified in the Army's business case for Increment 2, the Army has stated that additional development is necessary because LMP, as currently deployed, will not enable the Army to generate auditable financial statements. The National Defense Authorization Act for Fiscal Year 2010 required the development of a plan to ensure that the financial statements of DOD are validated as ready for audit not later than the end of fiscal year 2017.[14] LMP product office and AMC officials told us that the Army cannot meet this requirement with the functionality currently provided by Increment 1, and the Army's fiscal year 2013 and 2014 working capital fund budget documents state that

---

[14]Pub. L. No. 111-84, § 1003 (2009).

although LMP is functional at AMC's life cycle management commands, it requires the enhancements and upgrades of Increment 2 to generate auditable financial statements. In general, DOD considers the successful implementation of enterprise resource planning systems—which include LMP—critical to addressing long-standing weaknesses in financial and supply chain management, and DOD officials have stated that these systems are critical to ensuring that the department meets its requirement to have auditable consolidated financial statements.[15]

According to Army officials, a key LMP improvement in Increment 2 that supports audit readiness is the addition of the shop floor automation tool (part of the Enhanced Industrial Base component listed in table 2). The tool provides a standardized approach for managing shop floor operations across AMC's depots and arsenals. This tool, according to Army officials, will provide the capability to track the labor and material expenses to specific work tasks and customers, which is a more detailed reporting capability than what is currently provided by Increment 1. Army officials acknowledged that some locations such as Corpus Christi Army Depot have developed local tools to manage shop floor operations but asserted that such tools cannot support the Army's achievement of audit readiness. They stated that a significant investment of funds would be needed to make locally developed tools auditable, and that doing so would not be economically feasible.

In addition, according to Army officials, it would not be possible to gain all of the capabilities to be delivered with Increment 2 simply by upgrading legacy systems and modifying processes. For example, the Army is currently continuing to use one of the legacy systems that LMP was intended to replace—the Commodity Command Standard System—to control and maintain visibility over material managed by non-Army

---

[15]For a discussion of the role of enterprise resource planning systems in achieving financial audit readiness, see GAO, *DOD Financial Management: Reported Status of Department of Defense's Enterprise Resource Planning Systems*, GAO-12-565R (Washington, D.C.: Mar. 30, 2012).

sources of supply.[16] According to officials from the LMP product office and AMC, this legacy system cannot currently support the Army's need for auditable financial statements by fiscal year 2017 and thus needs to be replaced. By implementing this component of Increment 2, the Army expects to fully eliminate its need for the Commodity Command Standard System. Another example is related to item unique identification. According to DOD, financial management information necessary for the management of the department's mission critical assets is also required to support future financial statement audits.[17] This financial management information includes item unique identification, which cannot be accomplished using existing systems or through a completely manual process because, according to Army officials, some unique item identifiers are not human-readable. Instead, Army officials stated that AMC requires an electronic scanner that is planned to be included in the deployment of Increment 2. As a further justification for expanding LMP, the Army estimates that Increment 2 will cost $730 million through fiscal year 2026 but achieve approximately $1.4 billion in financial benefits.[18] Table 3 shows the financial benefits that the Army has projected for Increment 2.

---

[16]According to the Army's business case for LMP Increment 2, some inventory is owned by the Army yet managed by another organization, such as the Defense Logistics Agency. Because the Army does not manage this inventory, LMP is unable to search or reallocate this inventory to support other operations. Army documents also state that these processes were added to the Commodity Command Standard System after the initiation of LMP and that AMC decided in 2005 that this functionality would not be included in the initial deployment phases of LMP for reasons including time line and cost concerns.

[17]Office of the Under Secretary of Defense (Comptroller) and Chief Financial Officer, *Financial Improvement and Audit Readiness Guidance* (Washington, D.C.: Mar. 2013).

[18]We have included the projected benefits that are reported in the economic analysis that accompanies the Army's business case for LMP Increment 2 to demonstrate the magnitude of the financial benefits the Army expects to realize as a result of deploying Increment 2. We did not assess the business case's methodology or independently verify the reliability of the business case's results.

Table 3: Projected Financial Benefits from LMP Increment 2

Dollars in millions

Area of financial benefits	FY14	FY15	FY16	FY17	FY18 - FY26	Total
Reduced contractor support	-	-	-	20.1	523	543.2
Overtime reduction	-	-	-	7.0	182.2	189.2
Legacy information technology	-	2.0	9.6	16.4	156.0	183.9
National Maintenance Program	-	-	8.7	17.4	156.5	182.6
Legacy operations	-	-	4.7	11.8	89.5	106.1
Industrial operations personnel reduction	-	-	-	3.3	86.7	90.0
Item unique identification	-	5.5	5.5	5.5	49.9	66.5
Non-Army managed item inventory reduction	-	1.6	1.6	1.6	-	4.7
Total	**-**	**9.1**	**30.1**	**83.2**	**1,243.7**	**1,366.1**

Source: Army's LMP Increment 2 economic analysis.

Note: Total numbers may not add up, due to rounding.

The financial benefits shown in table 3 include both anticipated cost savings and cost avoidance. The Army is anticipating cost savings totaling approximately $1.1 billion from reduced contractor support, overtime, legacy information technology, legacy operations, and AMC industrial operations personnel. According to officials from the LMP product office and AMC, cost savings will be realized as reductions to the Army's planned budgets starting in fiscal year 2017. Officials cited an AMC memo which states that approximately $30 million of the cost savings from reduced contractor support, overtime, and AMC industrial operations personnel should be realized in fiscal year 2017; $60 million should be realized in fiscal year 2018; and $90 million should be realized in fiscal year 2019 and annually thereafter for the life of LMP.[19] According to the officials, the memo is referring to reductions in planned Army budgets in the specified fiscal years.[20] The approximately $250 million in remaining financial benefits expected from Increment 2 includes cost

---

[19]AMC, *Army Materiel Command (AMC) Logistics Modernization Program (LMP) Increment 2 Productivity Improvements*, Jun. 7, 2013.

[20]The memo states that the reductions will be time-phased to accommodate the expected learning curve before the productivity improvements are realized following the deployment of Increment 2. Additionally, the memo states that AMC industrial personnel will be reduced by attrition across the AMC industrial locations through the normal Army working capital fund rate-setting and workload management process.

avoidances from implementing the National Maintenance Program component of Increment 2, providing automatic item unique identification recording capability that will eliminate the need to manually perform those tasks, and reducing excess non-Army managed item inventory.

LMP Has Provided Some Benefits to the Army, but the Extent of Financial Benefits to Date Is Unknown

The use of LMP has provided the Army some benefits, but whether the system has delivered the expected financial benefits to date is unknown because AMC does not have a process to track these benefits. Since its deployment, LMP has provided some benefits to the Army. For example, because LMP relies on accurate data to perform effectively and efficiently, the Army has made data accuracy a priority. The Army has made progress in improving the accuracy of its data by conducting data assessments, correcting data problems, and placing management emphasis on data accuracy. Additionally, the use of LMP has improved accountability for inventory stored at AMC depots and has increased visibility over Army assets. However, the full extent of the financial benefits realized from LMP—which the Army projected would be over $750 million by the end of fiscal year 2012—is unknown because the Army has not tracked the benefits. Federal guidelines and standards outline the need for assessing whether expected benefits from an investment are achieved.[21] To support the development of Increment 2, the Army is developing a performance baseline for sites that will initially deploy Increment 2. Without a process in place to identify and document financial benefits linked to LMP-driven performance improvements, the Army will be unable to track whether it is achieving the expected financial benefits from its sizeable investment.

LMP Has Provided Some Benefits to the Army

Since its deployment, LMP has provided the Army some benefits. During our prior reviews of LMP before the final deployment phase had occurred, we reported that sites using LMP stated it was an improvement over legacy systems, because it increased visibility over assets and provided a

---

[21]See OMB, *Circular A-94: Guidelines and Discount Rates for Benefit-Cost Analysis of Federal Programs,* Oct. 29, 1992; OMB, *Capital Programming Guide: Supplement to Office of Management and Budget Circular A-11, Planning, Budgeting, and Acquisition of Capital Assets,* Jul. 2013; GAO, *Information Technology investment Management: A Framework for Assessing and Improving Process Maturity,* GAO-04-394G (Washington, D.C.: Mar. 2004); and GAO, *Standards for Internal Control in the Federal Government,* GAO/AIMD-00-21.3.1 (Washington, D.C.: Nov. 1, 1999).

single source of data for decision making.[22] During our visits to AMC headquarters and the 14 AMC sites for the current review, officials provided examples of various benefits resulting from using LMP, such as increased visibility over inventory and maintenance operations.

We also found that, since our prior reviews, AMC has made progress in improving the accuracy of LMP data that it uses to support industrial operations by conducting data assessments, correcting data problems, and placing management emphasis on data accuracy. Data accuracy is necessary in order for enterprise resource planning systems such as LMP to perform effectively and efficiently. For example, to support repairs of vehicles, LMP contains data that identify the number of vehicles scheduled for repair at a depot, the number of parts needed to support these repairs, and the capacity of the depot to perform the repairs. Based on these data, LMP will recommend to item managers that they purchase a specific quantity of spare parts by a certain date in order to support the scheduled repairs. In order for these recommendations to be correct, the data they are based on must be accurate. If the data on which they are based are not accurate, item managers may purchase either too many or too few spare parts, or the purchases may not be made in time to support the scheduled repair—which could lead to repairs not being completed according to the planned schedule. According to the AMC Data Integrity Strategy, a data accuracy rate of 95 percent or greater—depending on the type of data—is consistent with the industry standard.

The Army has instituted several processes to enhance data accuracy. A key effort involves periodic assessments at AMC sites to evaluate the accuracy of LMP data. AMC has determined that these assessments, which are conducted by its Logistics Support Activity, should focus on 29 critical data objects—groupings of data based on function—such as bills of material, purchase orders, or a sequence of repair activities. Between August 2010 and November 2012, the Logistics Support Activity performed 361 assessments across AMC that covered 18 of the 29 critical data objects. The results of these assessments are documented in reports, and the root causes of any problems are identified for correction. Logistics Support Activity officials stated that their goal is to focus attention on these root causes so that data problems do not continue to occur. They will then perform a follow-up assessment, if it is deemed

---

[22]GAO-11-139 and GAO-10-461.

necessary, to assess whether data accuracy has improved. For example, in August 2011, the Logistics Support Activity conducted a review of bills of material at various sites across AMC and assessed the accuracy of AMC's bills of material at 51 percent—well below their 95-percent standard. In a follow-up review conducted in May 2012, the Logistics Support Activity assessed the overall accuracy of AMC's bills of material at 92 percent. Furthermore, officials from the Logistics Support Activity stated that follow-up assessments at individual AMC sites have revealed improvements in data accuracy. For example, an initial assessment of work center data at the Letterkenny Munitions Center showed data accuracy to be 27 percent, while the follow-up assessment showed data accuracy to be 100 percent. Officials estimated that sites meet the 95-percent standard during initial data assessments only half of the time, but in follow-up assessments they meet the standard about 90 percent of the time.

AMC sites we visited are also performing their own internal reviews of LMP data accuracy. For example, Letterkenny Army Depot has a data quality team that has conducted a number of internal assessments. One of these assessments, conducted in October 2012 on the bill of material for a TOW missile, found that multiple materials were listed on the bill of material as required but had no or very limited consumption. Depot officials told us that, based on these types of assessments, the depot intends to make changes to its data to more accurately reflect usage of materials during repairs. Similarly, in order to assess and improve the data in LMP, officials at Anniston Army Depot mapped out the entire end-to-end repair process for the M9 Armored Combat Earthmover, which enabled them to identify data errors in LMP that they corrected. Officials at Red River Army Depot told us that they prepare weekly reports for depot management, and that data accuracy is discussed during meetings held by the depot commander. Officials also stated that they are emphasizing the importance of maintaining accurate LMP data and are holding users accountable for their management of LMP data. For example, officials at all five Army depots stated that LMP users and their supervisors are expected to ensure that the data they manage are accurate.

The use of LMP has also increased visibility over inventory. AMC officials stated that LMP provides the capability to automatically calculate the parts needed to conduct a repair at a depot. If the depot does not have these parts, LMP recommends that the needed parts be purchased from some other source of supply. In order for this process to work effectively, all inventory at the depot should be recorded in LMP so the system does not recommend ordering parts the depot already has. Officials at AMC sites we visited told us that prior to LMP, parts might be purchased by the Army and stored at the depot but not necessarily recorded in the legacy systems. Accordingly, item managers could make unnecessary purchases of inventory items that were available but not visible within the legacy systems. AMC stated that, due to the inventory reviews following the deployment of LMP and corrections made to inventory records, it entered more than $200 million worth of inventory into LMP that had already been purchased by the Army and was physically located at the depots but was not recorded in the legacy systems. Accordingly, AMC officials expect that officially tracking inventory that had already been purchased could result in a cost avoidance in the future. Similarly, Aviation and Missile Command officials stated that the better visibility of inventory in LMP enabled them to identify excess inventory that was on hand, which resulted in a cost avoidance of $1.2 million due to reduced inventory storage costs.[23]

The use of a single source of data provided by LMP, according to AMC officials, has resulted in other efficiencies. For example, officials at the AMC War Reserve Division stated that they are now able to provide near real-time updates to address questions on the status of war reserves to Army headquarters. These officials stated that, prior to LMP, the process to answer questions from Army headquarters would require 3 weeks to collect and analyze data from the life cycle commands; now, the process can be completed by extracting a report from LMP in minutes. Additionally, AMC officials stated that the single source of data has reduced the number of meetings that need to be held. For example, AMC officials who manage secondary inventory items stated that they are able to track the status of obligations across each of the life cycle management commands by extracting a consolidated report directly from LMP. The officials stated that, prior to LMP, they would hold bi-weekly meetings with the life cycle commands to capture the same information. Additionally, officials at Red River Army Depot stated that LMP provides visibility of inventory at all AMC locations, which has enhanced their ability to redistribute parts to support production needs. These officials stated that, prior to LMP, they had to call other depots to see if additional

---

[23]Aviation and Missile Life Cycle Management Command officials stated that the cost avoidance due to inventory storage costs was a result of disposing of $3 billion of inventory on hand that had already been purchased. We did not independently verify these estimates.

parts were available; with LMP, they are able to quickly identify which locations have the additional parts.

Finally, AMC officials stated that LMP has enabled them to develop and begin to implement a set of standardized, enterprise-wide performance measures to better assess the business operations of AMC sites. They told us that the measures previously used to assess AMC performance were inadequate, in part because they were not standardized. For example, officials stated that there was no standard measure for the rate of inventory turnover—which measures the number of times an inventory item is used and replaced during a given period—but that AMC was working on developing such a measure. At the time of our review, the standardized performance measures that AMC had developed included one for inventory turnover, as well as others for depot schedule performance, depot cost performance, forecast accuracy, supplier delivery performance, and direct versus indirect labor hours. According to documents provided by AMC, these measures were being used during regularly-held meetings with AMC headquarters beginning in June 2013.

Extent of Financial Benefits to Date from Deploying LMP Is Unknown

The extent to which expected financial benefits have been realized to date from deploying LMP is unknown, because AMC does not yet have a process to track these benefits. Without a process in place to track financial benefits associated with LMP, the Army does not have a way to determine whether LMP's projected financial benefits are materializing. The Army expected significant financial benefits from the deployment of LMP Increment 1 across AMC, which was completed in October 2010. According to a 2009 study prepared by the Army to support the fiscal year 2010 Investment Review Board certification of LMP, the system was expected to lead to over $750 million in financial benefits by fiscal year 2012 and eventually achieve more than two dollars in benefits for every dollar spent.[24] In its fiscal year 2014 budget documents, the Army projected that LMP would provide an estimated net financial benefit of nearly $1.3 billion through 2020. The Army expected these financial benefits to be achieved largely by LMP-driven improvements to the

---

[24]We have included the results of the Army's 2009 study to demonstrate the magnitude of the financial benefits the Army expected to realize as a result of deploying LMP. We did not assess the study's methodology or independently verify the reliability of the study's results.

performance of AMC operations through, for example, reducing inventory, improving productivity, and reducing costs for legacy systems.

Federal guidelines and standards outline the need for assessing whether expected benefits from an investment are achieved. According to the Office of Management and Budget's Circular A-94, which provides general guidance for benefit-cost analysis of federal programs, an element of benefit-cost analysis is verification of expected benefits.[25] The circular states that retrospective studies to determine whether anticipated benefits and costs have been realized are potentially valuable. Such studies can be used to determine necessary corrections in existing programs and to improve future estimates of benefits and costs in these programs or related ones. Agencies should have a plan for periodic, results-oriented evaluation of program effectiveness. They should also discuss the results of relevant evaluation studies when proposing reauthorizations or increased program funding. The Office of Management and Budget's Capital Programming Guide also states that a post-implementation review of an information technology project should evaluate an investment's efficiency and effectiveness to determine how well the investment achieved the planned functionality and anticipated benefits.[26] Additionally, GAO's Information Technology Investment Management framework states that a critical process for building a foundation for information technology investment success is providing investment oversight.[27] The purpose of this critical process is to ensure that the relevant organization provides effective oversight for its information technology projects throughout all phases of their life cycles. Such oversight should include observing the project's progress toward expected cost, schedule, and benefits. Furthermore, federal internal control standards state that managers should compare actual performance to planned or expected results throughout the organization and analyze significant differences.[28]

---

[25]*Circular A-94: Guidelines and Discount Rates for Benefit-Cost Analysis of Federal Programs.*

[26]*Capital Programming Guide: Supplement to Office of Management and Budget Circular A-11, Planning, Budgeting, and Acquisition of Capital Assets.*

[27]GAO-04-394G.

[28]GAO/AIMD-00-21.3.1.

However, the extent to which the Army has realized the expected financial benefits from LMP is unknown because AMC does not yet have a process to identify and document financial benefits realized as a result of performance improvements gained through the use of LMP. We asked AMC headquarters officials for information on the total financial benefits achieved from using LMP, but they were unable to provide such information because they could not quantify the impact LMP had on inventory value or provide measurements of improved productivity. Officials did not provide an explanation for why they did not have a process to track financial benefits, but they stated that the inability to quantify financial benefits from LMP-driven performance improvements was due in part to the fluctuations in AMC workload resulting from operations in Iraq and Afghanistan. Additionally, most AMC sites we visited reported that LMP had not led to financial benefits that they could quantify. Specifically, officials at 12 of the 14 sites we visited stated that LMP either had not resulted in any quantifiable financial benefits or that they could not provide us with any documentation that quantified the financial benefits.

The LMP product office and two AMC sites reported financial benefits from LMP. According to the LMP product office, an estimated $114 million of financial benefits were attributed to legacy system costs that were avoided through fiscal year 2012 as a result of LMP deployment. Additionally, in March 2013, the Aviation and Missile Command reported a $1.2 million cost avoidance due to reduced storage costs from the disposal of excess inventory. Finally, as noted earlier in this report, Corpus Christi Army Depot reported that use of LMP, in conjunction with a locally-developed software tool and manual processes, enabled it to improve depot processes and decrease the costs to repair UH-60 helicopters by approximately $760,000 per helicopter. Because 51 UH-60 helicopters were repaired in fiscal year 2012, AMC officials estimated a total cost savings of approximately $39 million.

LMP product office and AMC officials told us that there was not an accurate process currently in place to track financial benefits associated with LMP-driven performance improvements. Further, the officials stated that retroactively producing an accurate assessment of benefits realized to date from LMP would be difficult, because the Army had not established a baseline for performance prior to the implementation of LMP against which LMP-driven improvements could then be measured. The officials added that the Army has learned this lesson and has incorporated operational performance metrics in its plans for Increment 2. (These operational metrics are separate from the enterprise-wide performance measures discussed earlier in this report that AMC began to use in June 2013.) Specifically, the Army is in the process of developing an initial operational performance baseline for sites that will pilot Increment 2. According to documents provided by the LMP product office, these operational metrics include assessing the time needed to repair a weapon system or component; the direct labor charges needed to support production at industrial activities; program support overtime (i.e., the amount of overtime for indirect labor—such as schedulers, planners, and resource managers); data entry lag time; tracking the labor and materials expended for rework operations; and inventory visibility managed outside of LMP. Officials from the LMP product office and AMC stated that the process to baseline performance against these metrics is ongoing and primarily focused on the Increment 2 pilot sites, with the intention of assessing performance across all of AMC before the next milestone decision for Increment 2 in May 2015. Because the baseline is still under development, the degree to which these operational metrics will enable the Army to demonstrate financial benefits from deploying Increment 2 is unknown.

Conclusions

Over the last decade, the Army has made progress using LMP to support its industrial operations, has improved data accuracy in LMP, and has realized benefits. However, because the Army has not established a process for tracking LMP's financial benefits, it is not in a position to determine whether it is realizing a return on its sizeable investment in LMP. The Army plans to spend another $1.7 billion on operating the deployed components of LMP Increment 1 over the course of the system's life cycle, in addition to spending another $730 million on Increment 2. Given the magnitude of the investment already committed and planned to be committed to LMP, oversight by decision makers in DOD and the Congress would likely improve with a better understanding of what financial benefits have been realized from deploying LMP to determine whether the Army's goals for the system are being met and resources are being used effectively.

Recommendation for Executive Action

To determine whether the Army is achieving its estimated financial benefits in LMP, we recommend that the Secretary of Defense direct the Secretary of the Army to develop and implement a process to track the extent of financial benefits realized from the use of LMP during the remaining course of its life cycle. This process should be linked with the LMP performance baseline now being developed by the Army for use at AMC industrial sites.

Agency Comments and Our Evaluation

We provided a draft of this report to DOD for comment. The Army provided written comments, which are reproduced in appendix II. The Army concurred with our recommendation and stated that it will develop a process to track the extent of financial benefits recognized within LMP, which will be linked to the LMP performance baseline. The Army also stated that it is initiating a series of workshops to establish an enduring process to capture the financial benefits realized from the use of LMP. These actions, when implemented, will meet the intent of the recommendation. In addition, the Army provided technical comments, which we have incorporated as appropriate.

We are sending copies of this report to appropriate congressional committees, the Secretary of Defense, and the Secretary of the Army. In addition, this report will be made available at no charge on the GAO website at http://www.gao.gov.

Should you or your staff have any questions concerning this report, please contact me at (202) 512-5257 or merrittz@gao.gov. Contact points for our Offices of Congressional Relations and Public Affairs may be found on the last page of this report. GAO staff who made key contributions to this report are listed in appendix III.

Zina D. Merritt
Director
Defense Capabilities and Management

Appendix I: Scope and Methodology

To assess the extent to which LMP supports AMC's industrial operations, we met with officials at AMC headquarters responsible for overseeing LMP to discuss the system's deployment and usage. We reviewed our prior work related to the deployment of LMP and followed up on issues that we had previously identified. We also obtained and reviewed pertinent documents, including reports submitted to AMC headquarters by the life cycle management commands and subordinate sites on the status of their industrial operations. We met with officials at 14 AMC sites—including all five AMC life cycle management commands and all five AMC maintenance depots—where LMP is deployed. Specifically, we visited the following individual sites:

Life cycle management commands

- Army Sustainment Command, Rock Island, Illinois
- Aviation and Missile Command, Huntsville, Alabama
- Communications-Electronics Command, Aberdeen, Maryland
- Joint Munitions and Lethality Command, Rock Island, Illinois
- Tank-automotive and Armaments Command, Warren, Michigan

Maintenance depots

- Anniston Army Depot, Anniston, Alabama
- Corpus Christi Army Depot, Corpus Christi, Texas
- Letterkenny Army Depot, Chambersburg, Pennsylvania
- Red River Army Depot, Texarkana, Texas
- Tobyhanna Army Depot, Tobyhanna, Pennsylvania

Manufacturing arsenal

- Rock Island Arsenal (Joint Manufacturing and Technology Center), Rock Island, Illinois

Ammunition sites

- Anniston Defense Munitions Center, Anniston, Alabama
- Letterkenny Munitions Center, Chambersburg, Pennsylvania
- McAlester Army Ammunition Plant, McAlester, Oklahoma

We judgmentally selected Rock Island Arsenal to visit based on its proximity to the headquarters of Army Sustainment Command and the Joint Munitions and Lethality Command, McAlester Army Ammunition Plant based on the scope of its manufacturing and storage mission, and Anniston and Letterkenny Munitions Centers based on their proximity to

Army depots. During these site visits, we interviewed officials and obtained relevant documentation regarding the extent to which they used LMP to conduct their operations, were taking actions to improve the accuracy of the data used in LMP, and had realized nonfinancial and financial benefits from LMP.

We also obtained and analyzed Army documents, including the business case and an accompanying economic analysis, that were developed to support the Army's proposal to move forward with the development and acquisition of Increment 2. We met with officials from AMC headquarters and the LMP product office to discuss their plans for Increment 2, and we also discussed the Army's plans for Increment 2 with officials at individual AMC sites.

To determine the extent to which the Army has realized expected benefits from deploying the system, we obtained and reviewed Army documentation describing the expected benefits to be achieved from deploying LMP, including briefings describing the expected benefits and functionality of the system, a 2009 study supporting the fiscal year 2010 Investment Review Board certification of LMP, Army budget documents, and evidence that AMC headquarters, the individual sites, and the LMP Product Office were able to provide regarding actual benefits, if any, achieved to date. We also met with officials at AMC's Logistics Support Activity to discuss their efforts to improve the accuracy of data used in LMP, and we obtained and reviewed AMC's strategy for LMP data accuracy as well as documentation on LMP data accuracy assessments performed by the Logistics Support Activity. To assess the reliability of LMP data, we reviewed related documentation on LMP data accuracy and interviewed officials knowledgeable about LMP data. We determined the data were sufficiently reliable for the purposes of our report.

We conducted this performance audit from August 2012 to November 2013 in accordance with generally accepted government auditing standards. Those standards require that we plan and perform the audit to obtain sufficient, appropriate evidence to provide a reasonable basis for our findings and conclusions based on our audit objectives. We believe that the evidence obtained provides a reasonable basis for our findings and conclusions based on our audit objectives.

Appendix II: Comments from the Department of the Army

DEPARTMENT OF THE ARMY
OFFICE OF THE DEPUTY CHIEF OF STAFF, G-4
500 ARMY PENTAGON
WASHINGTON, DC 20310-0500

DALO-CIO

2 8 OCT 2013

MEMORANDUM FOR DIRECTOR, DEFENSE CAPABILITIES AND MANAGEMENT, U.S. GOVERNMENT ACCOUNTABILITY OFFICE, 441 G STREET, NW, WASHINGTON, D.C. 20548

SUBJECT: Response to Government Accountability Office (GAO) Draft Report Dated September 19, 2013, GAO-14-51 (GAO Code 351766)

1. This is the Department of Defense (DoD) response to the GAO Draft Report GAO-14-51, "Defense Logistics: Army Should Track Financial Benefits Realized from its Logistics Modernization Program," dated September 19, 2013 (GAO Code 351766).

2. The Department of Defense (DoD) acknowledges receipt of the draft report. We reviewed the draft and appreciate the GAO's support in identifying areas of improvement. Overall, DoD concurs with the GAO's recommendation.

3. The point of contact is Mr. Scott Larrabee, (703) 692-9034, or e-mail: scott.larrabee.civ@mail.mil.

Encl

RAYMOND V. MASON
Lieutenant General, GS
Deputy Chief of Staff, G-4

Government Accounting Office (GAO) Draft Report Dated SEPTEMBER 19, 2013
GAO-14-51 (GAO CODE 351766)

"DEFENSE LOGISTICS: ARMY SHOULD TRACK FINANCIAL BENEFITS
REALIZED FROM ITS LOGISTICS MODERNIZATION PROGRAM"

DEPARTMENT OF DEFENSE COMMENTS
TO THE GAO RECOMMENDATION

RECOMMENDATION 1: To determine whether the Army is achieving its estimated financial benefits in LMP, GAO recommend that the Secretary of Defense direct the Secretary of the Army to develop and implement a process to track the extent of financial benefits realized from the use of LMP during the remaining course of its life cycle. This process should be linked with the LMP performance baseline now being developed by the Army for use at AMC industrial sites.

DoD RESPONSE: Concur.

The Army concurs with the recommendation to develop a process to track the extent of financial benefits recognized within the Logistics Management Program (LMP), which will be linked with the LMP performance baseline. The Army will continue to reshape current metrics by leveraging the capabilities inherent in LMP. The Army is initiating a series of workshops to establish an enduring process to capture the financial benefits realized from the use of LMP. Financial benefits will be aligned to support the equipment supply, and readiness requirements and at the least risk to the Army's operational units.

Appendix III: GAO Contact and Staff Acknowledgments

GAO Contact

Zina D. Merritt, (202) 512-5257 or merrittz@gao.gov

Staff Acknowledgments

In addition to the contact named above, Thomas Gosling (Assistant Director), Cynthia Grant, Joanne Landesman, Jim Melton, Geoffrey Peck, Amie Steele, and Michael Willems made key contributions to this report.

Related GAO Products

DOD Financial Management: Reported Status of Department of Defense's Enterprise Resource Planning Systems. GAO-12-565R. Washington, D.C.: March 30, 2012.

Defense Logistics: Oversight and a Coordinated Strategy Needed to Implement the Army Workload and Performance System. GAO-11-566R. Washington, D.C.: July 14, 2011.

Defense Logistics: Additional Oversight and Reporting for the Army Logistics Modernization Program Are Needed. GAO-11-139. Washington, D.C.: November 18, 2010.

DOD Business Transformation: Improved Management Oversight of Business System Modernization Efforts Needed. GAO-11-53. Washington, D.C.: October 7, 2010.

Defense Logistics: Actions Needed to Improve Implementation of the Army Logistics Modernization Program. GAO-10-461. Washington, D.C.: April 30, 2010.

Defense Logistics: Observations on Army's Implementation of the Logistics Modernization Program. GAO-09-852R. Washington, D.C.: July 8, 2009.

DOD Business Transformation: Lack of an Integrated Strategy Puts the Army's Asset Visibility System Investments at Risk. GAO-07-860. Washington, D.C.: July 27, 2007.

Army Depot Maintenance: Ineffective Oversight of Depot Maintenance Operations and System Implementation Efforts. GAO-05-441. Washington, D.C.: June 30, 2005.

DOD Business Systems Modernization: Billions Continue to Be Invested with Inadequate Management Oversight and Accountability. GAO-04-615. Washington, D.C.: May 27, 2004.

DOD Competitive Sourcing: Plan Needed to Mitigate Risks in Army Logistics Modernization Program. GAO/NSIAD-00-19. Washington, D.C.: October 4, 1999.

GAO's Mission	The Government Accountability Office, the audit, evaluation, and investigative arm of Congress, exists to support Congress in meeting its constitutional responsibilities and to help improve the performance and accountability of the federal government for the American people. GAO examines the use of public funds; evaluates federal programs and policies; and provides analyses, recommendations, and other assistance to help Congress make informed oversight, policy, and funding decisions. GAO's commitment to good government is reflected in its core values of accountability, integrity, and reliability.
Obtaining Copies of GAO Reports and Testimony	The fastest and easiest way to obtain copies of GAO documents at no cost is through GAO's website (http://www.gao.gov). Each weekday afternoon, GAO posts on its website newly released reports, testimony, and correspondence. To have GAO e-mail you a list of newly posted products, go to http://www.gao.gov and select "E-mail Updates."
Order by Phone	The price of each GAO publication reflects GAO's actual cost of production and distribution and depends on the number of pages in the publication and whether the publication is printed in color or black and white. Pricing and ordering information is posted on GAO's website, http://www.gao.gov/ordering.htm. Place orders by calling (202) 512-6000, toll free (866) 801-7077, or TDD (202) 512-2537. Orders may be paid for using American Express, Discover Card, MasterCard, Visa, check, or money order. Call for additional information.
Connect with GAO	Connect with GAO on Facebook, Flickr, Twitter, and YouTube. Subscribe to our RSS Feeds or E-mail Updates. Listen to our Podcasts. Visit GAO on the web at www.gao.gov.
To Report Fraud, Waste, and Abuse in Federal Programs	Contact: Website: http://www.gao.gov/fraudnet/fraudnet.htm E-mail: fraudnet@gao.gov Automated answering system: (800) 424-5454 or (202) 512-7470
Congressional Relations	Katherine Siggerud, Managing Director, siggerudk@gao.gov, (202) 512-4400, U.S. Government Accountability Office, 441 G Street NW, Room 7125, Washington, DC 20548
Public Affairs	Chuck Young, Managing Director, youngc1@gao.gov, (202) 512-4800 U.S. Government Accountability Office, 441 G Street NW, Room 7149 Washington, DC 20548

Please Print on Recycled Paper.